ITALY

I0801760

By Jennifer Lombardo
and Alicia Z. Klepeis

EXPLORING
WORLD
CULTURES

Cavendish Square

Published in 2024 by Cavendish Square Publishing, LLC
2544 Clinton Street, Buffalo, NY 14224

Copyright © 2024 by Cavendish Square Publishing, LLC

Second Edition

No part of this publication may be reproduced, stored in a retrieval system, or transmitted in any form or by any means—electronic, mechanical, photocopying, recording, or otherwise—without the prior permission of the copyright owner. Request for permission should be addressed to Permissions, Cavendish Square Publishing, 2544 Clinton Street, Buffalo, NY 14224. Tel (877) 980-4450; fax (877) 980-4454.

Website: cavendishsq.com

This publication represents the opinions and views of the author based on their personal experience, knowledge, and research. The information in this book serves as a general guide only. The author and publisher have used their best efforts in preparing this book and disclaim liability rising directly or indirectly from the use and application of this book.

All websites were available and accurate when this book was sent to press.

Library of Congress Cataloging-in-Publication Data

Names: Lombardo, Jennifer, author. | Klepeis, Alicia, 1971- author.
Title: Italy / by Jennifer Lombardo and Alicia Z. Klepeis.
Description: Second edition. | Buffalo, NY : Cavendish Square Publishing, [2024] | Series: Exploring world cultures | Includes bibliographical references and index.
Identifiers: LCCN 2023029723 | ISBN 9781502669933 (library binding) | ISBN 9781502669926 (paperback) | ISBN 9781502669940 (ebook)
Subjects: LCSH: Italy--Juvenile literature.
Classification: LCC DG417 .K54 2024 | DDC 945--dc23/eng/20230630
LC record available at https://lccn.loc.gov/2023029723

Writers: Alicia Z. Klepeis; Jennifer Lombardo (second edition)
Editor: Jennifer Lombardo
Copyeditor: Danielle Haynes
Designer: Andrea Davison-Bartolotta

The photographs in this book are used by permission and through the courtesy of: Cover Arsenie Krasnevsky/Shutterstock.com; pp. 4, 6 StevanZZ/Shutterstock.com; p. 5 Peter Hermes Furian/Shutterstock.com; p. 7 saiko3p/Shutterstock.com; p. 8 Sidhe/Shutterstock.com; p. 9 Alvaro German Vilela/Shutterstock.com; p. 10 Felix Lipov/Shutterstock.com; p. 11 Alessia Pierdomenico/Shutterstock.com; p. 12 muratart/Shutterstock.com; p. 13 Creative Lab/Shutterstock.com; p. 15 (top) topotishka/Shutterstock.com; p. 15 (bottom) Kwadrat/Shutterstock.com; p. 16 Vasilii L/Shutterstock.com; p. 17 Evgenyrychko/Shutterstock.com; p. 18 Kamira/Shutterstock.com; p. 19 volkova natalia/Shutterstock.com; p. 20 Mostovyi Sergii Igorevich/Shutterstock.com; p. 21 Buffy1982/Shutterstock.com; p. 22 imagestockdesign/Shutterstock.com; p. 23 Roman Babakin/Shutterstock.com; p. 24 marcobrivio.photography/Shutterstock.com; p. 25 (left) francesco de marco/Shutterstock.com; p. 25 (right) Pecold/Shutterstock.com; p. 26 George Rudy/Shutterstock.com; p. 27 Boerescu/Shutterstock.com; p. 28 Maya Pantic/Shutterstock.com; p. 29 norikko/Shutterstock.com.

Some of the images in this book illustrate individuals who are models. The depictions do not imply actual situations or events.

CPSIA compliance information: Batch #CW24CSQ: For further information contact Cavendish Square Publishing LLC at 1-877-980-4450.

Printed in the United States of America

Find us on

CONTENTS

INTRODUCTION

The European country of Italy has given the world many wonderful things. It's known for its food, art, buildings, and more. If you've ever eaten spaghetti or pizza, you've had a taste of Italian food!

People have lived in Italy for a long time. Different people have ruled Italy during its history. For many years, the country was one small part in a large **empire**. Today, it's a **republic**. People have many different kinds of jobs there. Some people work in hotels or schools. Others make clothes or grow food on farms.

The countryside in Italy is very good for farming. There are many vineyards, or grape farms.

Italy has mountains, islands, forests, and rivers. People from all over the world come to see Italy's beautiful scenery. They also visit its many cities. The people of Italy value good food, the arts, and music. Many famous artists have been born in Italy. Italians also love to have fun. They throw many parties and spend a lot of time with family and friends.

This map shows Italy, its islands, and the countries around it.

GEOGRAPHY

The main part of Italy is a **peninsula** shaped like a high-heeled boot. Italy also includes two islands called Sicily and Sardinia. The country is surrounded by several bodies of water. These include the Tyrrhenian Sea, the Adriatic Sea, and the Mediterranean Sea.

COUNTRIES IN A COUNTRY

Italy is the only country in the world with two other countries inside it: Vatican City and San Marino. Vatican City is ruled by the Catholic Church. San Marino, Europe's third-smallest country, is on top of a mountain toward the north of Italy.

The country of San Marino (shown here) covers 24 square miles (62 square kilometers) and has a population of about 34,000.

The Po River cuts through the city of Turin.

FACT!

*Italy has three active **volcanoes**. They're named Etna, Vesuvius, and Stromboli.*

Italy has many mountains and rivers. Its longest river is the Po River. It flows for 405 miles (652 km) across northern Italy. The Apennine Mountains run down Italy's center. They divide the country into east and west. The Alps are mountains that stretch across northern Italy.

All of Italy is hot and dry in the summer. Winters are comfortable in the south of the country, but cold and wet in the north.

HISTORY

People have lived in Italy for about 8,000 years. By the 700s BCE, a group called the Etruscans controlled central and northern Italy. The Greeks controlled southern Italy.

FACT!

Because Greece and Italy are so close to each other and have been part of each other's empires at certain points in time, parts of their ***cultures*** *are very similar.*

The Etruscans were some of Italy's earliest people. No one is sure where they first came from. Later, the Romans took over Italy and other nearby areas to create a powerful empire. At its largest

This map shows the Roman Empire at its largest.

and most powerful, the Roman Empire covered all the lands around the Mediterranean Sea. It ended in 476 CE, when German groups took over.

In 1861, Italy became one country under King Victor Emmanuel II. Kings ruled Italy until 1946. Italy then became a republic and remains one today.

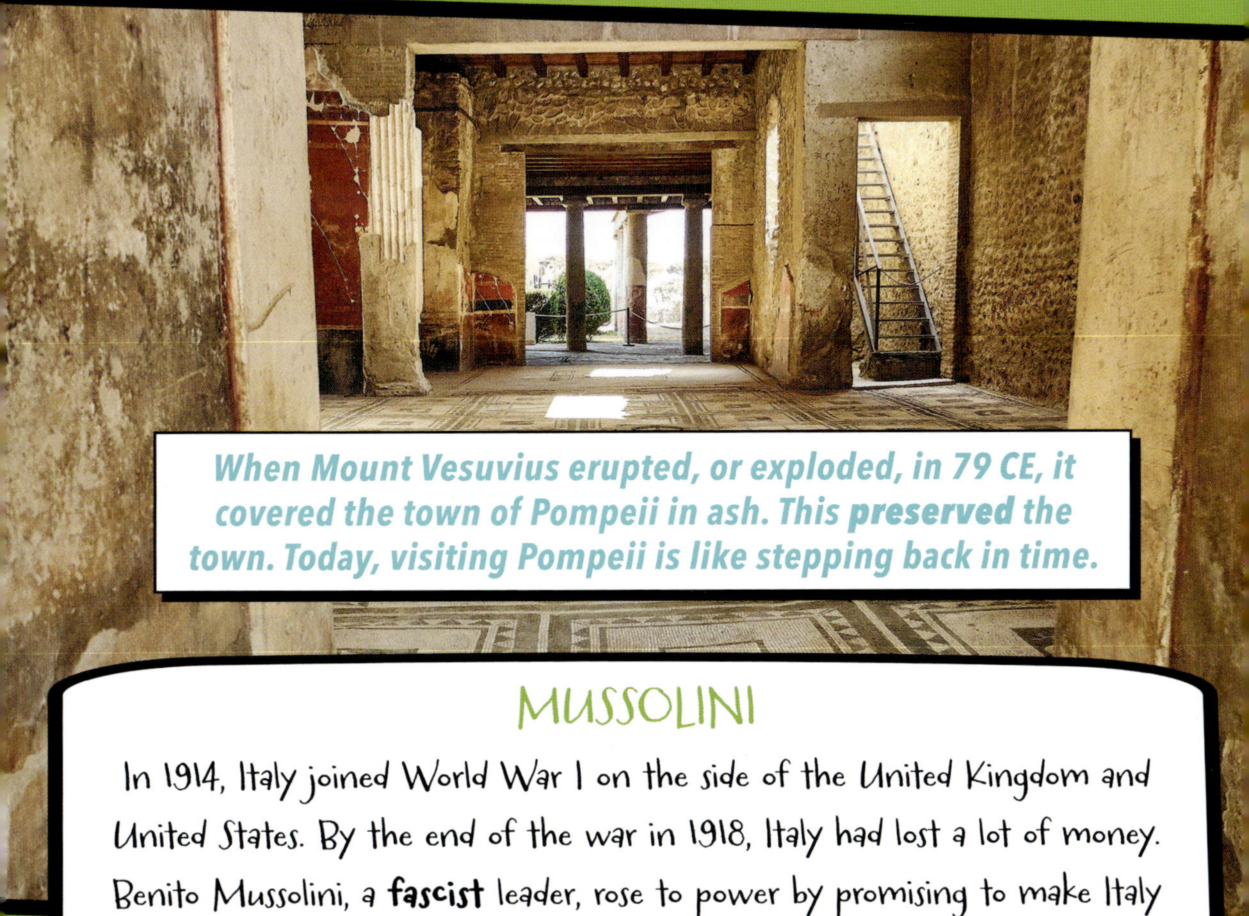

*When Mount Vesuvius erupted, or exploded, in 79 CE, it covered the town of Pompeii in ash. This **preserved** the town. Today, visiting Pompeii is like stepping back in time.*

MUSSOLINI

In 1914, Italy joined World War I on the side of the United Kingdom and United States. By the end of the war in 1918, Italy had lost a lot of money. Benito Mussolini, a **fascist** leader, rose to power by promising to make Italy an empire again. Toward the end of World War II (1939–1945), his enemies captured and killed him.

GOVERNMENT

The country of Italy is split into 20 parts called regions. Each has a capital city and a regional government, similar to the way each state in the United States has its own government. Rome is the capital of the country.

FACT!

Just like in the United States, Italians vote for their leaders, and the leaders then make the laws.

The Senate meets in the Palazzo Madama in Rome to pass laws.

Italy's government has three parts called branches. Parliament, the legislative branch, makes the laws. It's made up of two parts: the Senate and the Chamber of Deputies. The executive branch carries out the laws and makes sure people follow the laws. The judicial branch, which is made up of the courts, decides what the laws mean and what should happen to people who break them.

ITALY'S EXECUTIVE BRANCH

The president, prime minister, and **cabinet** members make up Italy's executive branch. The prime minister does most of the same things a U.S. president does. The Italian president mainly has a **ceremonial** job.

Italians elected Giorgia Meloni to be the country's first female prime minister in 2022.

THE ECONOMY

After World War II, Italy's **economy** grew quickly. Today, it has one of the largest economies in Europe. Italian factory workers make many different things, including cars, clothing, and stoves. Italy is well known for its nice (and expensive) shoes and clothes.

FACT!

Italian automakers build cars such as Ferraris, Lamborghinis, and Maseratis and ship them all over the world.

In the city of Venice, many of the streets are waterways called canals! Many tourists like riding through the canals on a kind of boat called a gondola.

Italian farmers grow many different crops. Some of the most important are grapes, olives, tomatoes, and sugar beets. Many people consider Italian meats and cheeses, such as prosciutto and mozzarella, to be some of the best in the world.

Tourism, or travel, is a big part of Italy's economy. Many Italians have jobs in hotels and as tour guides, showing people around the country.

The city of Milan is known for its fashion. Since 1958, the city has held a famous fashion show twice a year.

AFTER COVID-19

Italy's economy was hit very hard when COVID-19 started spreading around the world. However, the government made some good decisions, and most people chose to get **vaccinated**. This helped the economy bounce back quickly.

THE ENVIRONMENT

Many countries around the world, including Italy, are facing problems with their environment, or natural world. Some Italian factories make the nearby air, soil, and water polluted, or dirty. Cars can also cause pollution, especially in cities with a lot of drivers.

Many different plants and animals are found in Italy. Some of the animals there include wolves, brown bears, and golden eagles. There are also many fish, but overfishing and pollution are putting some kinds of sea life in danger. Plants such as olives and strawberries are native to the country.

The people and government of Italy are trying to make their country cleaner. One way they're doing this is by using solar, or sun, power. Solar power doesn't pollute the air.

FACT!

The world is getting warmer because of human actions. Italy, which is already a hot country, is having problems with this extra heat.

Rosemary is a plant that's native to Italy. It's used in many Italian dishes.

ROMULUS AND REMUS

The wolf is an important symbol, or sign, of Italy. An old story says a mother wolf raised two human brothers, Romulus and Remus. Romulus grew up and created the city of Rome, which he named after himself.

The greyhound is an Italian racing dog.

THE PEOPLE TODAY

As of 2023, Italy's population is almost 59 million. About 71 percent of Italians live in cities. The three biggest cities are Rome, Milan, and Naples. Most of the people are native Italians. There are also groups of German-, French-, and Slovene-Italians living in northern Italy, where Italy shares its border with those countries.

FACT!
More than 4 million people live in Rome.

Rome is famous for its architecture, or buildings. This picture shows the remains of the Colosseum. Ancient Romans came here to watch deadly fights for fun.

In the southern part of the country, there are many Albanian-Italians and Greek-Italians. Each group has blended its own culture with Italian culture, which means life is a little different all over the country. However, no matter where they come from, Italians are very proud of their country and culture.

AVOIDING A PROBLEM

Even though Italy is close to Africa, the country has a big problem with **racism**. Some Italians treat Black people poorly. However, many Italians pretend there is no racism in Italy. This means they aren't working to fix it.

Italians are known for "talking" with their hands. For example, when food is very good, they may kiss the tips of their fingers to show they love it. This is called a "chef's kiss."

LIFESTYLE

Life in Italian cities is very different than life in the countryside. In the city, an Italian might live in a modern apartment building or a house that's hundreds of years old. Some use cars or scooters to get around. Others ride the bus or subway. Most Italians have computers and cell phones.

WOMEN IN ITALY

In the past, Italian women stayed home to take care of their house and children. Today, many women have jobs outside of the home. However, many Italian men have had a hard time letting go of old ideas about what women can do.

People who live in Venice get around on a vaporetto, or water bus.

People living in the country often raise animals and grow crops for food. Houses in the countryside are spread farther apart than in the cities. Most people live in small towns. A few live alone in the hills, with no other people around for miles.

FACT!

Italians take a three-hour break called riposo during the hottest part of the day. Workplaces close, and people often go home to eat and rest.

In the country, some Italians live in large houses called villas.

RELIGION

About 80 percent of Italians are Christian, and most of those Christians are Roman Catholic. The two biggest Christian holidays are Christmas and Easter. Many towns and villages in Italy have special days, called feast days, for Catholic saints, or holy people.

Religion, or faith, is changing in Italy. Before 1984, Catholicism was Italy's official religion. This means the country made laws based on Catholic beliefs. Today, Italy has a separation of religion and government.

This picture shows Florence's most famous Catholic church.

Babies become part of the Catholic Church in an event called baptism. In recent years, some Italians have started "de-baptizing" themselves because they realized as adults that they don't believe in what the Church teaches.

FACT!

The Roman Empire was the birthplace of the Christian religion.

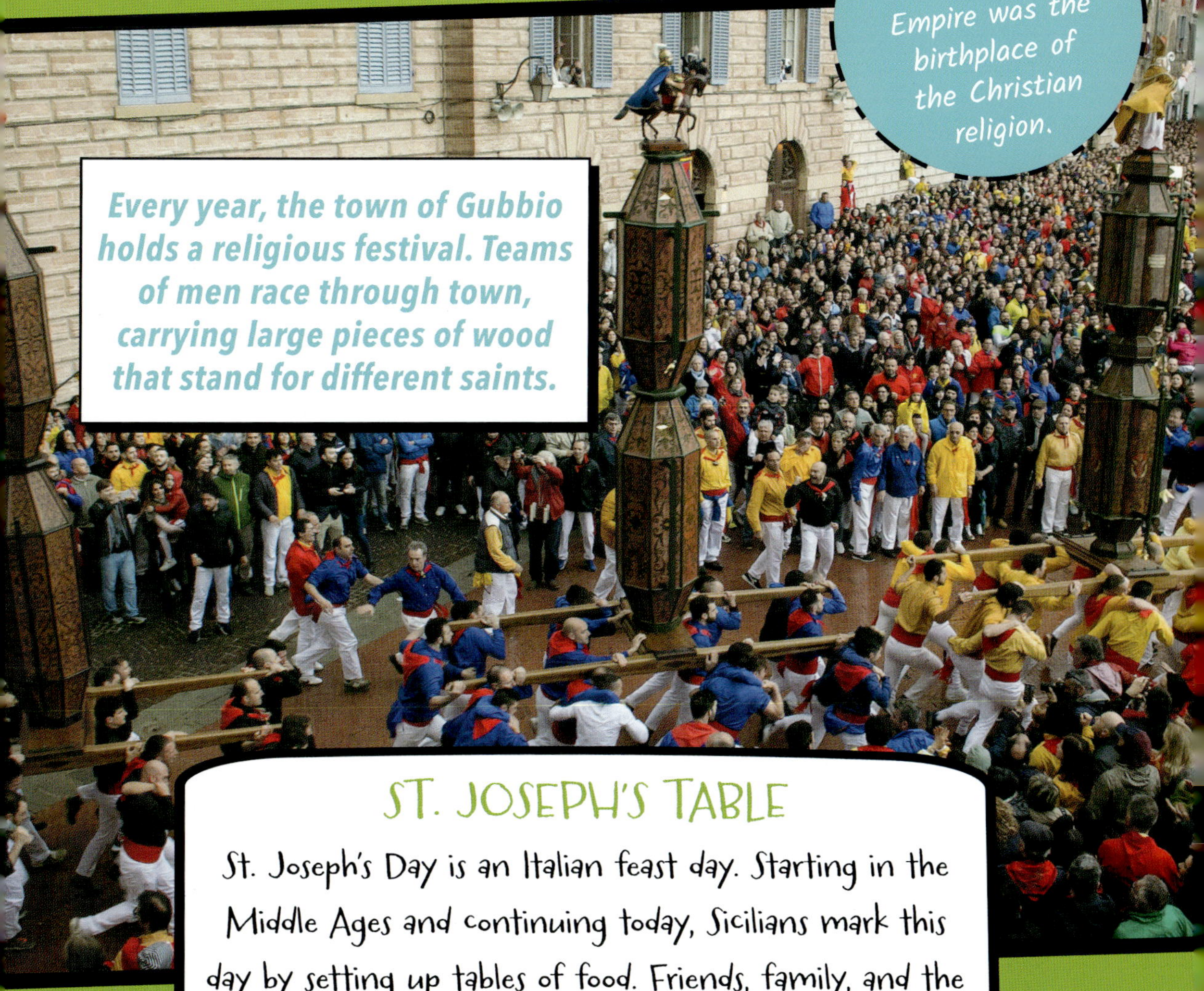

Every year, the town of Gubbio holds a religious festival. Teams of men race through town, carrying large pieces of wood that stand for different saints.

ST. JOSEPH'S TABLE

St. Joseph's Day is an Italian feast day. Starting in the Middle Ages and continuing today, Sicilians mark this day by setting up tables of food. Friends, family, and the community are invited to eat. No one is turned away.

LANGUAGE

In ancient Rome, people spoke Latin. Over time, this became the base for many languages, including the Italian that people speak today. Italian is Italy's official language. This means it's used by the Italian government as well as schools and businesses across the country. Almost everyone in the country speaks Italian.

FACT!

People who live on the Italian island of Sardinia have their own language called Sardinian. It's the closest to ancient Latin of any modern language.

The ancient Romans had their own system of numbers. These are still used all over the world today. This chart shows how to read them.

Roman Numerals

1 = I	10 = X	100 = C	1000 = M
2 = II	20 = XX	200 = CC	2000 = MM
3 = III	30 = XXX	300 = CCC	3000 = MMM
4 = IV	40 = XL	400 = CD	
5 = V	50 = L	500 = D	
6 = VI	60 = LX	600 = DC	
7 = VII	70 = LXX	700 = DCC	
8 = VIII	80 = LXXX	800 = DCCC	
9 = IX	90 = XC	900 = CM	

In some parts of Italy—especially the parts that border other countries—people speak other languages. These include German, Greek, and French. Immigrants, or people who move to Italy from other countries, also bring their own languages with them.

Many Italians learn to speak more than one language. Most schools teach English as a second language.

BORROWED WORDS

Over hundreds of years, travel and immigration have led to many world languages borrowing words from each other. Some Italian words English has borrowed include volcano, tarantula, and piano. English words Italian has borrowed include sandwich, chat, and weekend.

In Rome, many street signs are on the sides of buildings. Via means "street."

ARTS AND FESTIVALS

Italy is the home of some of the most famous art in the world. During a period of time called the Renaissance from the 14th to 17th century, Italian artists created works of art that people still enjoy today.

FACT!
Italians invented Christmas carols.

It took Michelangelo a little more than four years to paint the walls and ceilings of the Sistine Chapel in Vatican City in the early 1500s.

TURTLES AND ARTISTS

The Teenage Mutant Ninja Turtles are named after four Italian Renaissance artists: Michelangelo Buonarroti, Leonardo da Vinci, Raffaello Sanzio (known as Raphael), and Donato de Betto di Bardi (known as Donatello).

Italians created a style of musical theater called opera in the early 1600s. Like other Italian inventions, it has spread around the world and is still popular today. However, Italians like all kinds of music, including rap and pop.

Italy has a number of national holidays. One that is unique, or special, to Italy is Liberation Day on April 25. Italians hold parades and concerts to remember when the country became free from German control after World War II.

Every year, Venice hosts a big party called Carnival. People decorate gondolas and wear fancy clothes and masks.

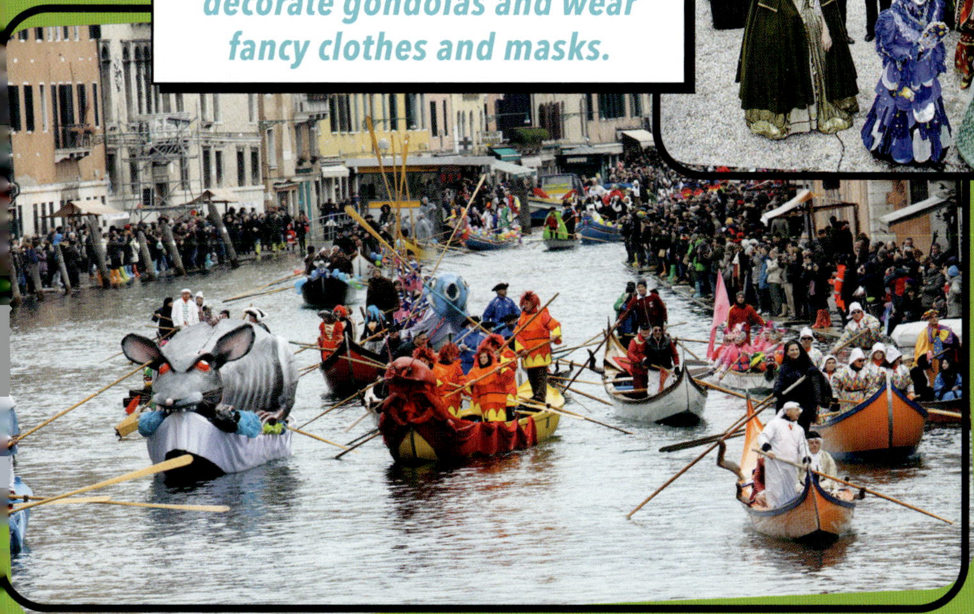

FUN AND PLAY

Soccer—or football, as many countries call it—is popular all over the world. However, Italians love it more than most! Some famous soccer teams from Italy are AC Milan, Napoli, and Juventus.

Italians enjoy many other sports too. In the winter, some people go skiing or sledding in the mountains. Swimming and bicycling are also popular. Many Italians also like to watch Formula One Grand Prix car racing.

Italians say they invented foosball, or table football. While this may not be true, Italy does make and sell the most foosball tables today.

Many Italian games have been around in one form or another for thousands of years. Every September in Verona, there's a festival where people play ancient street games. However, Italians also enjoy modern video and board games.

TAROT CARDS

In the 1440s, people in Milan, Venice, Florence, and Urbino started recording the rules of a card game called tarocchi. It became popular and spread to France, where they renamed it tarot. In the late 1700s, some French men started using tarot cards to **predict** the future, which is what they're known for today.

FACT!

The Romans may have invented hopscotch. They also played a game called piastra, which changed over time into a modern-day game called bocce.

There are many places to ski in the Italian Alps.

FOOD

Italians love good food, and having coffee or a meal is a common way for people to spend time with their loved ones.

Because the water is so close, Italians eat a lot of fish. People also enjoy many kinds of meat, such as ham and lamb. They

FACT!

Many people think of tomato sauce as being a big part of Italian food. However, tomatoes are native to South America. They weren't used in Italian cooking until the mid-1500s.

Espresso is very strong coffee. Italians have many different ways of preparing it.

often mix meat or fish with pasta. There are many kinds of sauces that go with pasta. These include creamy sauces, such as alfredo, and oil-based sauces, such as pesto. Mushrooms and artichokes are two frequently used vegetables.

Cooks use seasonings such as rosemary, basil, and garlic in many dishes. Desserts often feature fruits such as peaches, plums, apricots, and oranges, which grow well in Italy.

FROM CHINA TO ITALY

The Chinese were the first to create noodles. Through trade, they made their way to Italy by the 13th century. The Italians changed how the noodles were made. The new noodles, known as pasta, became a unique Italian food.

Shown here are some common Italian dishes.

GLOSSARY

cabinet: The group of people that gives advice to the political head of a government.

ceremonial: Having no real power.

culture: The beliefs and ways of life of a certain group of people.

economy: The way goods and services are made and sold.

empire: A group of lands and peoples under one ruler.

fascist: Relating to a political system led by a dictator in which the government controls everything and opposition is not allowed.

peninsula: A piece of land surrounded on three sides by water.

predict: To guess what will happen in the future.

preserve: To keep free from decay or destruction.

racism: The practice of treating others poorly because they are part of a different race, or group.

republic: A country governed by elected representatives and an elected leader.

vaccinated: Given a shot to keep a person safe from a certain illness.

volcano: A vent in the Earth's crust from which melted rock and steam come out.

FIND OUT MORE

Books

Brink, Tracy Vonder. *Italy*. New York, NY: Crabtree Publishing, 2022.

Murray, Julie. *Italy*. Minneapolis, MN: Abdo Kids, 2023.

Sabelko, Rebecca. *Italy*. Minneapolis, MN: Bellwether Media, 2023.

Websites

Kids World Travel Guide: Italy
www.kids-world-travel-guide.com/italy-facts.html
Read more about Italy, and take a look at some amazing pictures.

***National Geographic Kids*: Italy**
kids.nationalgeographic.com/geography/countries/article/italy
Learn more interesting facts about Italy's history, geography, and culture.

Video

YouTube: The Animated History of Italy (Part 1)
www.youtube.com/watch?v=Y16QLJOVP6s
Learn about how the Roman Empire became the modern-day country of Italy.

Publisher's note to educators and parents: Our editors have carefully reviewed these websites to ensure that they are suitable for students. Many websites change frequently, however, and we cannot guarantee that a site's future contents will continue to meet our high standards of quality and educational value. Be advised that students should be closely supervised whenever they access the internet.

INDEX